Guided reading notes

by Kate Ruttle (series editor)

Trackers level 4: Parrot tracks

Zounds Sounds

Genre: non-fiction   **Text type:** puzzle   **Author:** Sarah Fleming

Have you ever wondered how sounds are made or why different instruments make different sounds? Can you draw a picture of a sound? Read the information, solve the puzzles and find the answers to your questions.

High frequency words	Useful long vowel phonemes	Content words and Tricky words
by, different, down, into, long, other, right, round, why	'aw' in *about, cow, down, loud, round, sound* 'ee' in *beads, being, either, key, machine, mouthpiece, people, wheel* 'ie' in *inside, higher, kind, likely, synthesise, why*	*although, electric, choir, description, either, guitar, instrument, percussion, piece, rhythm, synthesiser, vibration*

Guided reading

The aim of this series is to encourage children to read for meaning. This booklet provides page-by-page notes suggesting a variety of ways to do this.

Guided reading could be covered in three stages:

1 Introduce the book
2 Read the book
3 Revisit the book

For guidance on how to go through these stages, see the back cover.

Main text is black text on a white background. This is the text that the children should try to read independently. It contains a high proportion of high frequency and phonically regular words.

Other texts present a higher level of challenge, but most children should be able to read it with some support.

Independent reading

This book can be used for independent reading. To help children read for meaning, use some of the ideas from the 'Read the book' notes on the back cover.

Asking questions

Encourage the children to ask questions of you and of each other as both asking and answering questions develops comprehension. Throughout their reading, use the italicised questions in this booklet to make children think about the meaning of both individual words and bigger text.

Phonics and high frequency words

In the 'Follow on' boxes there is information about phonically regular words on the pages. If children get stuck on these words, they can be encouraged to 'sound them out'. The high frequency words listed are all from the *Trackers* Parrot Tracks high frequency word list (see Teacher's Guide) and are words that children need to learn to recognise.

For notes on phonics and high frequency words plus general information on how to teach these, see *Trackers* Teacher's Guide for levels 3 and 4.

How to use this booklet

This booklet is intended to support children in guided reading sessions. On each page in this booklet there is a page map, a diagram of the pupil's page, which represents a double-page spread (two pages) in the pupil's book. However, on page 3 of this booklet there might be information about pages 1–3 of the pupil's book. Page 14 includes information about pupil's book pages 22–24. On the page map, the page numbers (folios) refer to pages in the pupil's book.

The page map is annotated with these boxes:

Answer

From page 4 onwards in *Zounds Sounds*, the answer to the 'turn over question' is shown at the top left-hand side of the double-page spread. Other answers are on pages 22–24 of the pupil's book.

Heading

In *Zounds Sounds*, each new spread is a puzzle. The headings give a context for each picture on the pages.

Main text boxes

The main text is the larger text in the pupil's books. Any potentially challenging words will be identified in the initial 'vocabulary check'. Strategies for reading these words are suggested in the 'follow on' section. These include questions and ideas you can use to monitor children's understanding. Use these as a menu of suggestions rather than as a set list of questions.

Secondary text

The secondary text is the smaller text in the pupil's book. These contain supplementary information or questions.

Turn over question

In *Zounds Sounds* this question predicts the topic on the next page. The answer is over the page.

Developing comprehension skills

On page 15, there are some comprehension questions which will require the children to think beyond the scope of a double-page spread. These are consistent with the assessment focuses in SATs papers and include:
★ retrieval of detail (SATs assessment focus 2);
★ inference and interpretation (SATs assessment focus 3);
★ structure and organisation of text (SATs assessment focus 4);
★ writer's uses of language (SATs assessment focus 5);
★ writer's purpose and viewpoint and the overall effect of the text (SATs assessment focus 6).

SATs assessment focus 1 refers to the decoding strategies children use. Opportunities for assessing these are given in the follow on section on every double page.

Developing speaking and listening

Use the making meaning suggestions on each double-page spread to develop speaking and listening skills. These questions, and others in the 'Main text boxes', are often open-ended and support children as they develop their ideas and understanding through talk and discussion.

The main features of the text

Use the information on this page of this booklet to draw children's attention to the specific features of the text type used in the book. As their reading skills develop, it is important that children understand how different text types are structured. This will help them read more effectively and also to understand how texts work when they are writing.

Zounds Sounds is a puzzle text in which children have to read and interpret text and pictures in order to answer questions.

Text purpose

★ To encourage reading, thinking and observation skills by asking the reader to find information in different ways to answer questions.

Text structure

There is a new puzzle on each double-page spread. Information the children will need to solve the puzzle can usually be found on the spread.

Each has the same structure and uses a variety of sentence types:

★ *Statements* – these provide information and give the context for the puzzle questions.
★ *Questions* – these form the basis of the puzzle.
★ *Instructions* – these tell you what to do to solve the puzzles.
★ *Picture* – either a photograph or an illustration which needs to be interpreted.
★ The spreads are organised around families of instruments.
★ *Answers* – these are written in the form of statements on pages 22–24.

Sentence and word level features

★ *Written in the present tense* – puzzles of this sort are usually in the present tense, because the reader is doing the puzzles in the here and now.
★ *Puzzle text mostly consists of questions.* The puzzle works through asking questions of the reader. Most of the questions are closed questions, to which there is only one correct answer. This is because the nature of puzzle texts is that there should be 'right' and 'wrong' answers.
★ *Puzzle texts ask specific questions* whose answers can be found in the text rather than drawing on children's general knowledge.
★ *Context text* – is mostly presented as non-chronological report text, in the present tense and referring to general, not specific subjects. There are some instructions, drawing the reader's attention to specific features of the picture or text.

Pages 2 and 3

1 Heading
★ What do children know about sound waves?

2 Main text
★ vocabulary check: *vibrations*
★ Find out if the children recognise that this text is in the form of statements. It is like a report text in that it gives general information.

3 Main text
★ vocabulary check: *instruments*
★ Find out if the children recognise this instruction text. It is telling the children what to so that they can solve the puzzle question.

5 Puzzle text and picture
★ This is the puzzle question for this spread. The children need to read and understand the information given so far in order to know how to answer this question.

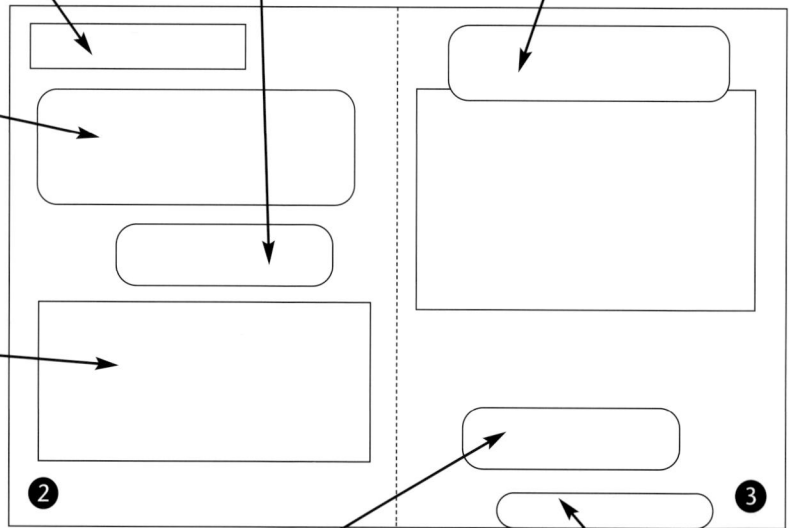

4 Labelled pictures
★ Talk about these sound waves. *How are they different? What do they have in common?*

2

3

6 Main text
★ vocabulary check: *synthesiser, real*
★ Remind the children that synthesisers are used in keyboards and computers to imitate sounds. The sound waves of the copied instrument are analysed and then reproduced by a computer.

7 Turn over question
★ This instrument uses synthesised sound. Do the children know what it is?

> **Follow on**

Tricky words
★ *vibrations* (The tricky bit is –*tion* representing 'shon'. Split into syllables: *vib-ra-tions*.)
★ *instruments* (Ask the children to split the word into syllables: *in-stru-ments*.)
★ *synthesiser* (Pronounce as: *sin-tha-size-er*.)
★ *real* (The tricky bit is *ea* appearing to be split over a syllable boundary. This only occurs before an *l*. Link to meal, seal, deal.)

Words and sentences
★ Can the children find three kinds of sentence:
  – statements, e.g. 'Synthesizers copy the sound waves made by real instruments.'
  – instructions, e.g. 'Now look at this sound wave.'
  – questions, e.g. 'What do you think this is?'

Making meaning
★ Ask the children to explain how the sound waves on page 2 are made. They should refer to the main text on page 2 to help them.

4

Pages 4 and 5

8 Answer to turn over question.
★ vocabulary check: *answer, electric, violin*
★ *How do you think an electric violin is similar to or different from an acoustic violin?*

9 Heading
★ vocabulary check: *musical*
★ *What is a musical family?* Make sure that the children understand that instruments are often categorised into families of instruments which make similar kinds of sounds in similar ways.

12 Puzzle text and pictures
★ Remind the children about why each of the instruments is classified into that family before they attempt to answer the questions.

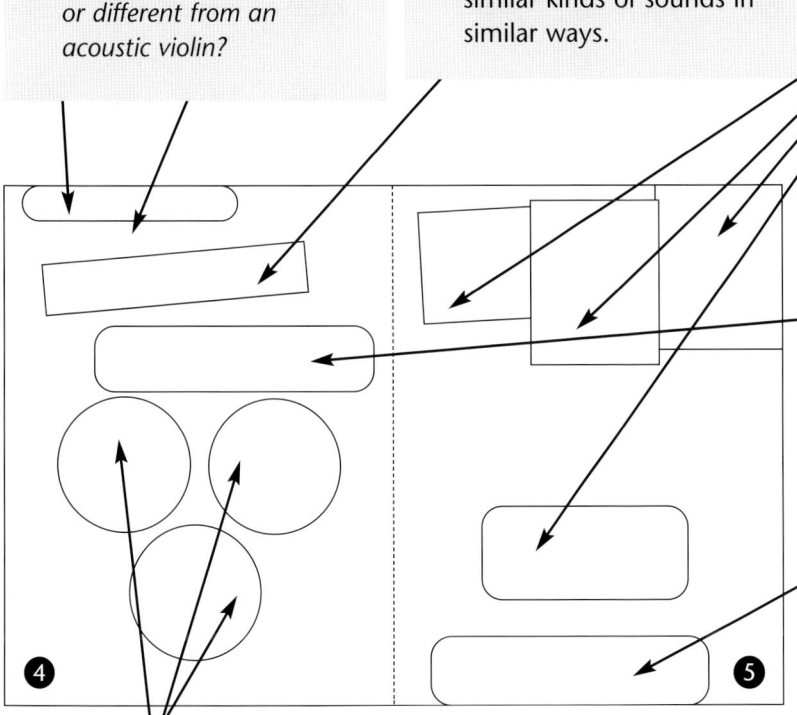

10 Text
★ vocabulary check: *percussion*
★ Talk about the musical family sets. See if the children recognise all the instruments.

13 Turn over question
★ vocabulary check: *piano*
★ Find out if the children know how a piano is played and ask if they know what is inside it. They will need to consider these issues to answer the question.

❹ ❺

11 Pictures
★ Can the children explain why each family is called by their name? (answer: You play *wind* instruments by blowing air through or over them; you play *string* instruments by making the strings vibrate; you hit *percussion* instruments to make them vibrate. The word *percussion* comes from the Latin *percussio*, meaning 'to strike'.)

⤳ Follow on ⤳

Tricky words
★ *answer* (The tricky bit is the silent *w*. Split into syllables: *ans-(w)er*.)
★ *electric* (Ask the children to split the word into syllables: *el-ec-tric*.)
★ *violin, piano* (The tricky bit is recognising the different pronunciation of the *i*. Split into syllables: *vi-o-lin* and *pi-a-no*.)

★ *musical* (Teach base word and adjective forming suffix *al*: *music* + *al*.)
★ *percussion* (The tricky bit is <u>ssion</u> representing 'shon'. Split into syllables: *per-cu-ssion*.)

Words and sentences
★ Look at the words which begin each of the questions. Ask the children to keep a tally chart showing which

words occur most often at the beginning of questions.

Making meaning
★ Ask the children to name other instruments that could be placed into each of the sets. See if they can explain their choices?

5

Pages 6 and 7

14 Answer to turn over question
★ Ask the children whether they know the answer.

15 Heading
★ *Have there been any instruments like this before? Look back at page 4.*

16 Subheading
★ Discuss the use of subheadings as indicating subsets of the heading.
★ *What is the other subheading on the page?*

17 Main texts
★ *So why is a piano called a string instrument?*

18 Subheading
★ vocabulary check: *bowed*
★ Ask the children if they know what a bow is. See if they can mime using one across the strings of an instrument.

20 Main text
★ vocabulary check: *double bass*
★ *Have you seen a double bass being played?*
★ Explain that different pieces of music need different bass sounds. In an orchestra, the double bass is often bowed; in jazz ensembles it is more often plucked.

19 Main text
★ *Why do you think bowing an instrument makes longer noises?*

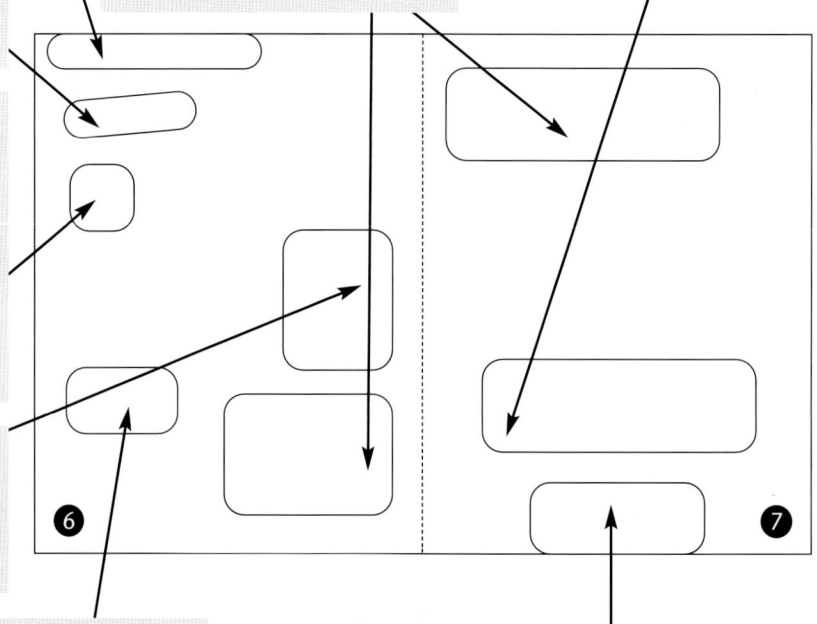

21 Turn over question
★ If the children can work out the answer to this question, they will be able to predict what they will find on the next page.

⓺   ⓻

> **Follow on**

Tricky words
★ *double* (The tricky bit is *ou* representing 'u'. Split into syllables: *dou-ble.*)
★ *bass* (This is a unique word. It's a homophone with base.)
★ *bowed* (The tricky bit is the confusion with the homograph. Rhyme *bow* with *low*. Teach base word and *ed*: *bow + ed.*)

Words and sentences
★ Find out how many comparative adjectives the children can find. (answer: *thicker, longer, softer*). Is *hammer* also a comparative adjective? Why not?

Making meaning
★ *In which other musical set could a piano be put? Discuss whether the piano could also be classified as a wind or percussion instrument.*

Pages 8 and 9

24 Puzzle question and pictures
★ The children do not need to name the guitars.
  - 1 is an electric base guitar
  - 2 is a national acoustic guitar
  - 3 is a folk acoustic guitar
  - 4 is an electric guitar
  - 5 is a Spanish acoustic guitar
★ The children will need to look carefully at the guitars on page 8 to spot the details.

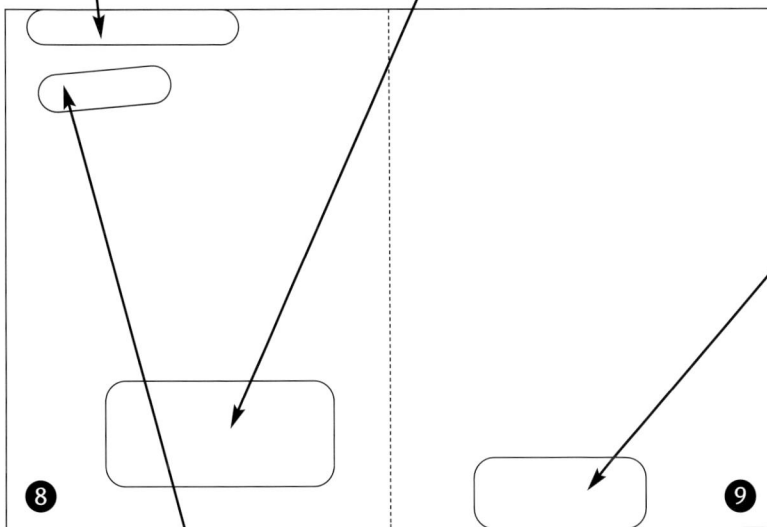

22 Answer to turn over question
★ vocabulary check: *guitar*
★ *Why would you use a guitar pick?*

25 Turn over question
★ If the children can't answer the question, can they at least work out how they are played? *Are they string, percussion or wind?*

8   **9**

23 Subheading
★ *Why is there no heading on this page?* (answer: this is still about the string family, so another heading is unnecessary)
★ Find out if the children know what 'plucking' means. Ask the children to mime how to do it on an air-guitar/ violin/ cello etc.

Follow on

Tricky words
★ *guitar* (the tricky bit is the silent *u* which is silent to prevent softening the *g*. Ask the children to split the word into syllables: *gui-tar*.)

Words and sentences
★ *Which question on this page could be answered with a simple 'yes' or 'no'? Would that be a helpful answer?*

Making meaning
★ Discuss why different guitars might be used for different kinds of music.

★ *Why couldn't you play a guitar with a bow?* (answer: Look at the shape of the bridge which keeps the strings high off the wood of a violin. The bridge separates the strings so that different angles of bowing play on a different string. Compare this to the flat look of guitar strings.)

Pages 10 and 11

26 Answer to turn over question
★ Ask the children if they can remember how percussion instruments are played.

27 Heading
★ *Why do we need a new heading here?*

28 Main text and pictures
★ Talk about the way the sounds the instruments make are shown. See if the children can pronounce them all?
★ *If a tuning fork isn't a musical instrument, what is it?* (answer: Wind, string and some percussion instruments need to be 'tuned', so that when they all play a note it sounds at exactly the same pitch. Tuning forks are used to create a constant note – usually A above middle C.)

29 Puzzle text
★ **vocabulary check:** *descriptions, rhythm/ rhythmic, shakere, covered, ratchet, piece, jagged, vibraslap, agogo, guiro, scraper*

30 Turn over question
★ *If the children can work out the answer, can they predict the topic of the next page?*

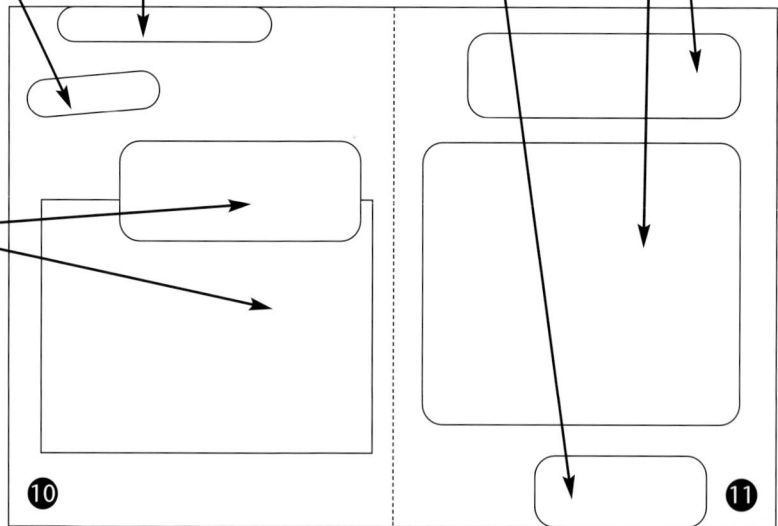

❿   ⓫

Follow on

Tricky words
★ *description* (The tricky bit is the *e* pronounced as 'i' and <u>tion</u> representing 'shon'. Split into syllables: *des-crip-tion*.)
★ *rhythm/ rhythmic* (Teach as a whole word: *rhythm* and as a base word and the adjective forming suffix *ic*: *rhythm + ic*.)
★ *shakere* (A unique word. Pronounce as: *shake-ear-y*.)
★ *covered* (The tricky bit is *o* being pronounced as 'u'. Teach base word + *ed*: *cover + ed*.)

★ *ratchet* (Ask the children to split the word into syllables: *ratch-et*.)
★ *piece* (The tricky bit is *ie* representing the long vowel sound 'ee'. Link to field.)
★ *jagged* (Teach base word and *ed*: *jag(g) + ed*.)
★ *vibraslap* (Separate the compound word into its components: *vibra + slap*.)
★ *agogo* (Pronounce the *go* as in *go*! Split into syllables: *a-go-go*.)
★ *guiro* (Pronounce as: *g-why-row*.)

★ *scraper* (Teach base word and suffix *er*: *scrape + er*.)

Words and sentences
★ Talk about the presentation of the definitions. Each one begins with the name of the instrument. *What else do they all include?*

Making meaning
★ Find out if the children can define 'musical instrument'? Discuss why a tuning fork is not a musical instrument.

Pages 12 and 13

31 Answer to turn over question
★ *Which continent do bongo drums come from?* (answer: Africa)

34 Subheading
★ *What do you think the roll of drums is in a group of musicians?* Drums usually give a constant beat or rhythm.

32 Puzzle text
★ **vocabulary check:** *timpani, mallet*
★ *Why would each of these drumsticks make a different sound?* Ask the children to think about the material on each of the stick heads.
★ *Which of the drums in the drum kit would you play using any of these sticks?*

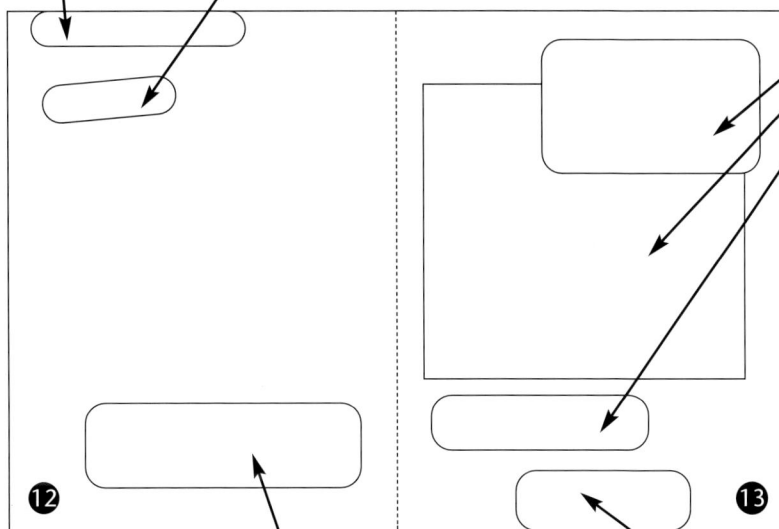

⑫   ⑬

33 Main text
★ *Can the children point to all the drums in the drum kit?*
★ *Why are there other instruments in addition to drums?*
★ *What is the pedal for?*

35 Turn over question
★ *This is only part of an instrument.* Remind the children of the musical families on pages 3 and 4. Which family do they think this might be from?

Follow on

Tricky words
★ *timpani* (Ask the children to split the word into syllables: *tim-pan-i.*)
★ *mallet* (Ask the children to split the word into syllables: *mall-et.*)

Words and sentences
★ *How many words can you find on these pages containing the word drum?* Talk about how the different words are constructed.

Making meaning
★ *When are drums played? How many different ways can the children think of?* (pop music, marching bands, drum music, different kinds of world music, orchestral music)

Pages 14 and 15

36 Answer to turn over question
★ vocabulary check: *mouthpiece*
★ *What do you think you do with a mouthpiece?* (answer: you blow through it) *What kind of instrument needs a mouthpiece?*

37 Heading
★ *Why do we need a new heading now?*

38 Subheading
★ Do the children know what brass is? Explain that it is a yellow/brown coloured metal. Can they suggest why all the instruments on this page might be called brass instruments?

39 Puzzle text and pictures
★ vocabulary check: *trombone*
★ The children will need to look carefully at the pictures on the page to solve the puzzle.

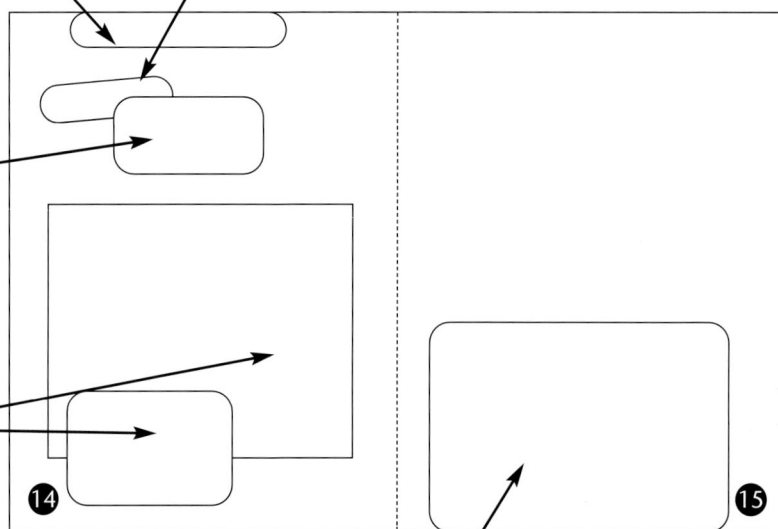

40 Turn over question
★ vocabulary check: *saxophone*
★ *Which family of instruments are these instruments in?*

⑭ ⑮

Follow on

Tricky words
★ *mouthpiece* (Ask the children to separate the compound word into its component words: *mouth + piece*.)
★ *trombone* (Ask the children to split the word into syllables: *trom-bone*.)
★ *saxophone* (Ask the children to split the word into syllables: *sax-o-phone*.)

Making meaning
★ *Do you think the mouthpieces of these instruments would be very different? Why?*
★ *Why do you think brass instruments need mouthpieces?* (answer: Different mouthpieces are slightly different sized to match the mouths of the players. Brass players change the notes on their instruments by changing the shape of their mouths, so it is important that the mouthpiece 'fits' the musician.)

10

Pages 16 and 17

41 Answer to turn over question
★ *Did you work it out correctly? What clues did you use?*

42 Subheading
★ **vocabulary check:** *woodwind*
★ *What do you think instruments in the woodwind family are made out of?*

43 Main text
★ **vocabulary check:** *although, plastic*
★ *Why might woodwind instruments be made of plastic?* (answer: Plastic is cheaper and it also stays in tune longer than wood which swells and shrinks as it gets hot and cold.)

44 Main text
★ **vocabulary check:** *clarinet*
★ If children have never seen a flute being played, liken the playing of a flute to blowing across the top of a bottle. If possible, compare the sounds and notice that the flute, like a bottle, makes a breathier sound than instruments you blow straight into.

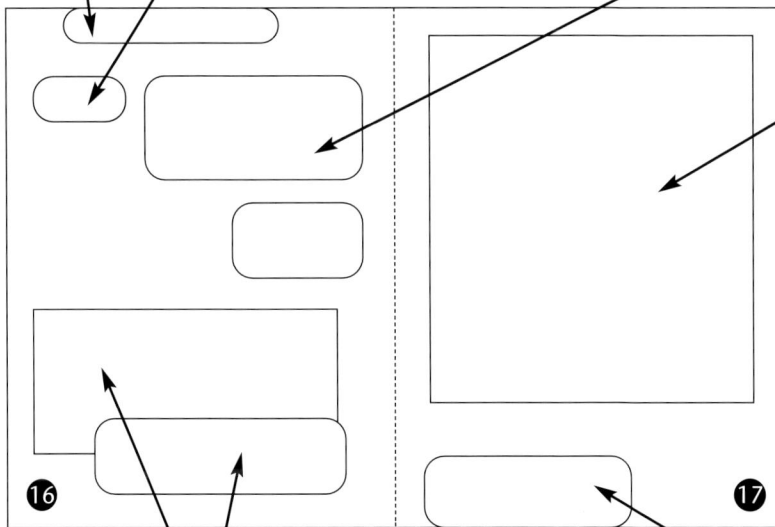

16 **17**

45 Main text
★ If children haven't played the kazoo, tell them that you don't blow into a kazoo – you hum with the kazoo in your mouth and the kazoo amplifies the humming sound to make a sort of tuneful buzzing.

46 Turn over question
★ Does the picture help the children to guess what the next instrument might be?

Follow on

Tricky words
★ *woodwind* (Separate the compound word into its components: *wood + wind*.)
★ *although* (The tricky bit is <u>ough</u> pronounced to rhyme with *blow*.)
★ *plastic* (Ask the children to split the word into syllables: *plas-tic*.)
★ *clarinet* (Ask the children to split the word into syllables: *clar-i-net*.)

Words and sentences
★ *Can you suggest an alternative name for woodwind instruments which are not made of wood?*

Making meaning
★ Ask the children to consider all the instruments on this page. *Which do you think would be the higher pitched? Which would be lower? Why?*

Pages 18 and 19

47 Answer to turn over question
★ **vocabulary check:** *voice*
★ *Did you know your voice could be called an instrument?*

48 Heading
★ *Why do we need a new heading?*

49 Main text
★ **vocabulary check:** *diagram, vocal, chord*
★ Point out that vocal cords are shorter when they are tighter, and longer when they are looser. Link this to all that children already know about pitch and size.

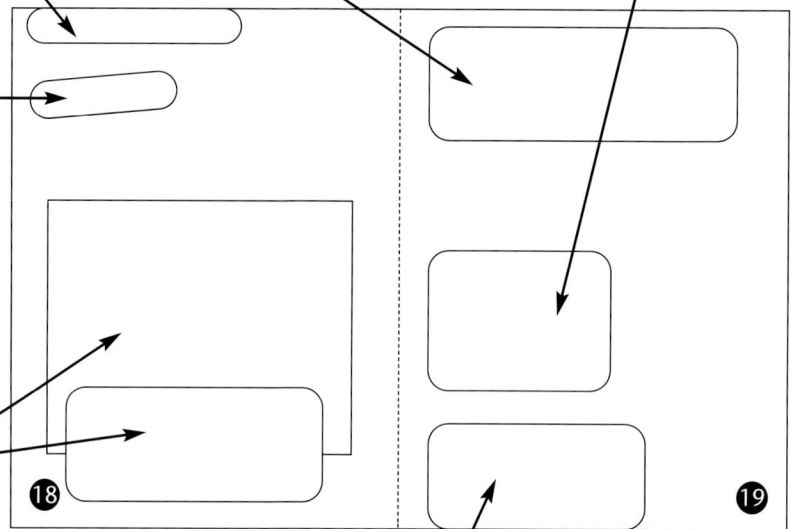

50 Main text
★ *Do the longer lines show louder or softer sounds?*

51 Puzzle text
★ Encourage children to follow the sound wave with their finger as they sing or hum the note. This will help you to know whether they understand the point. (NB Make sure the children don't confuse these sound waves with showing pitch – they just show volume.)

18 **19**

52 Turn over question
★ The children need to look carefully at the picture. There are a number of different words for people who sing together, but what does the picture show?

Follow on

Tricky words
★ *diagram* (The tricky bit is the syllable boundary between *i* and *a*. Ask the children to split the word into syllables: *di-a-gram*.)
★ *vocal* (Ask the children to split the word into syllables: *vo-cal*.)

Making meaning
★ Revisit the conversation you had earlier about what makes a musical instrument. Did the children's definition allow for voice to be included? Do they want to change it?

Pages 20 and 21

53 Answer to turn over question
★ **vocabulary check:** *choir*
★ *Is there a choir in your school? Where do you usually expect to see or hear choirs?* (answer: in churches or concert halls)

54 Heading
★ *Why do we need a new heading?*

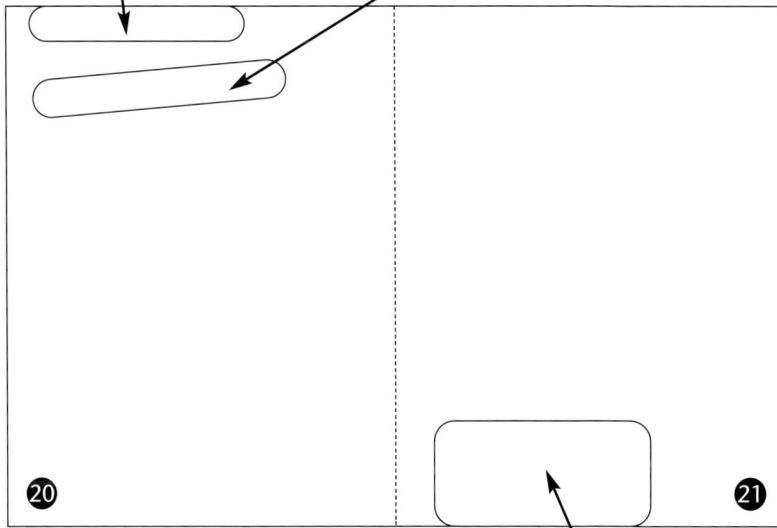

55 Turn over question
★ Ask the children to look back at pages 4 and 5.

Follow on

Tricky words
★ *choir* (This is a unique word. Teach the children to pronounce it: *k-why-er*.)

Pages 22, 23 and 24

56 Answer to turn over question

★ Spoons can be played as instruments. Ask
the children to think of other objects which
can be played as instruments. Look at the
photo on page 22.

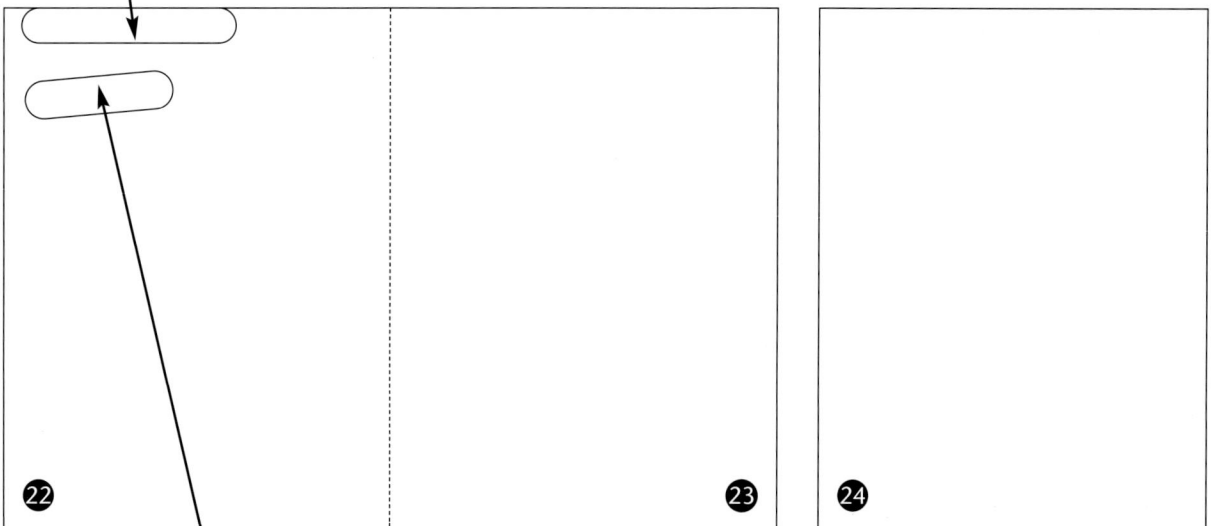

②②

②③ ②④

57 Answers

★ These pages contain the answers given to the questions asked in main
text, including puzzle text. The answers are all secondary text, so the
children may need help to read them.
★ Main text answers are on white backgrounds and secondary text answers
are on blue backgrounds.
★ Talk about the pictures on these pages. Ask the children if they can
describe the instruments?
★ You can use a bow to play a saw. Does this make it a string instrument?
★ See if the children can answer the last question on page 24.

Revisit the book

★ These questions are intended to make the children think about what they have understood from reading the book.

★ They are not intended to be used as a 'test', nor is it anticipated that children should answer all the questions.

★ First, ask the children to think back and try to answer the questions from memory. Then ask them to find the evidence in the text by finding words or pictures to support their answers.

Retrieval of detail

★ *Can you remember how many families of musical instruments were identified in the book? Look at the content page to check your answers.*

★ *What are sounds? (page 2)*

★ *What kind of instrument is a piano? Why? (page 6)*

★ *How many ways can you play a string instrument? (pages 6–8)*

★ *How many ways can you play a percussion instrument? (pages 10–11)*

★ *How many families of wind instrument are there in the book? (pages 14–17)*

★ *Which instrument do we always carry with us? (page 18)*

Inference and interpretation

★ *How do you think the names of the instrumental families are decided?*

★ *Why might you sometimes pluck violin strings rather than bow them?*

★ *Why don't all percussion instruments make the same sound?*

★ *What kinds of materials can you make wind instruments out of?*

★ *Why might people like to mix up the different kinds of instruments?*

Structure and organisation of text

★ *How is each of the pages organised? What kind of information does the heading give?*

★ *How did the author use the turn over questions?*

Author's uses of language

★ *How many different kinds of sentence does the author use? Why?*

Author's purpose and viewpoint and the overall effect of the text

★ *What is this book about? What is the author trying to make the reader do?*

1 Introduce the book

★ *What do you think this book is going to be about?* Discuss title, blurb and cover images.
★ *How many different ways do you know of playing musical instruments?*
★ *How does this book work?* Talk about the overall 'shape' of the book. Use the contents page and point out that, after an introduction, the book explores different families of musical instruments.
★ *Look at the way each page is set out.* Point out:
  – Headings
  – Main text identification – black text on a white background
  – Puzzle text
  – Turn over questions
  – Answers.

2 Read the book

★ As the children read, use questions and guidance on the spread-by-spread notes in this booklet, pages 4–14, and the questions children asked in the introductory session. Children can read either just main text, or they can attempt some of the more challenging secondary text.
★ Encourage the children to spend time considering the pictures – they can learn a lot from 'reading the pictures'.
★ At the end of the session, talk about what the children have found in response to the questions you asked.

3 Revisit the book

★ *Have your questions been answered?* Remind children of the questions they asked in the first session. Discuss which have been answered and ask the children why they think some of the questions may not have been answered.
★ *If another group were to read this book, which questions should they be asked to think about?* Encourage the children to re-read parts of the book independently to think about appropriate questions.
★ *How did you read the 'tricky words'?* Focus on tricky words and discuss children's strategies for decoding them.

Follow on

Use these for '5' minute' session beginnings or endings, or to focus children's attention on word, sentence or text level issues.
★ **'Tricky words'** suggests strategies for decoding words identified in the main text as being potentially challenging.
★ **'Words and sentences'** focuses on issues to do with vocabulary choice, punctuation, grammar and text layout.
★ **'Making meaning'** draws attention to bigger questions that arise from the text or pictures and help to develop comprehension.

OXFORD
UNIVERSITY PRESS

© Oxford University Press
First published 2004

www.OxfordPrimary.com

Zounds! Sounds!

Contents

Sarah Fleming

OXFORD
UNIVERSITY PRESS

Sound waves

Sounds are vibrations in the air. We hear things when air moves up and down very quickly, making a sound wave.

Look at the sound waves made by these three instruments:

trumpet

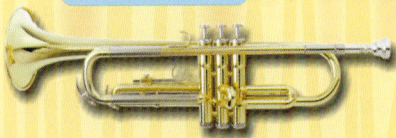

Attack – the start   Peak – the loudest part

Decay – from the peak until there is silence

electric guitar

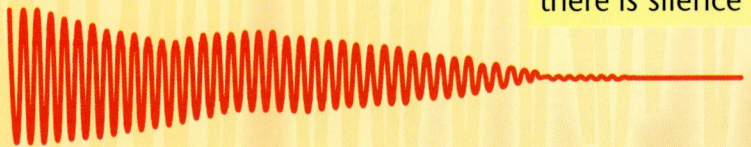

bongo drum

Now look at this sound wave. Which of these instruments do you think made it?

violin

snare drum

trombone

CLUE

Instruments that make the same kinds of sounds have the same kinds of sound waves.

Synthesizers copy the sound waves made by real instruments.

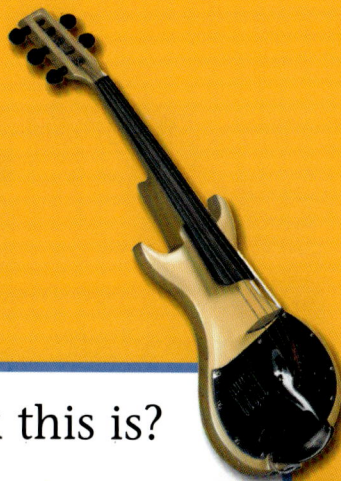

What do you think this is?

3

Musical sets

You can put most musical instruments into one of these sets:

Wind

oboe

Wood and Brass

penny whistle

saxophone

sousaphone

Percussion

castanets

drum

String

violin

zither

Wind instruments make sounds by blowing wind over or through them.

Percussion instruments vibrate when they are hit to make sounds.

String instruments make sounds by being bowed, plucked, strummed or hammered.

?2 Can you think of any instruments that don't fit into any of these sets?

tuba

guitar

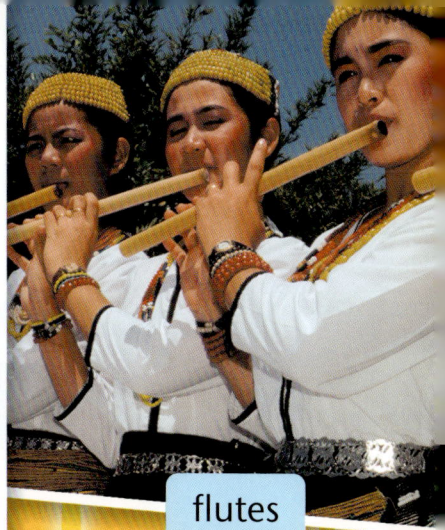

flutes

?3

Which sets would you put these instruments in?

?4

Look at this glockenspiel. Which bars make the lowest and the highest notes?

▶▶

What kind of instrument is a piano? Which set would you put it in?

Strings

There are lots of wire strings inside a piano. When you press a key, a hammer hits a string.

Hit

wire strings

keys

hammers

?5

Look at the strings. When the strings get longer and thicker, does the sound get lower or higher?

Compare the ways that the glockenspiel on page 5 and the piano (above) make notes sound higher or lower

Bowed

You can play some string instruments with a bow. This can make longer, softer noises.

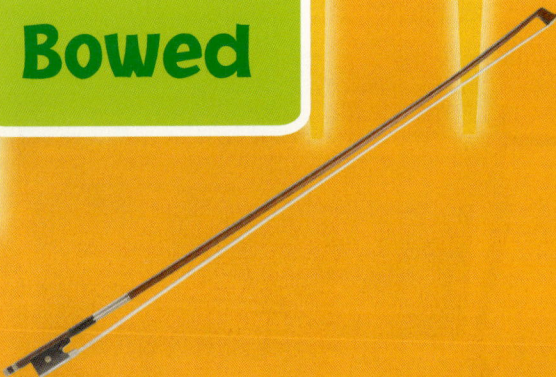

Which of these instruments plays the highest notes? Which one plays the lowest notes?

violin

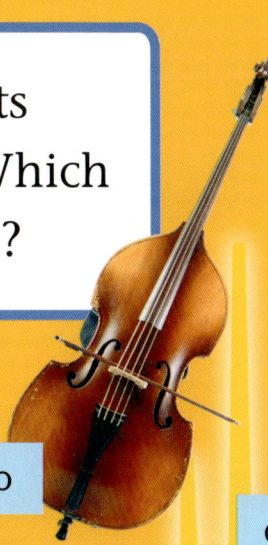

cello

double bass

?7

The double bass can be bowed or plucked. What difference do you think bowing or plucking makes to the sound?

▶▶

What are these?
What are they for?

Plucked

harp

These instruments are made to be plucked.

1 2 3 4 5

?8

Here are some different guitars. Which ones are electric?

8

A **B**

?9

Can you match these pictures with the different guitars on page 8?

?10

Look at these two guitars, can you spot two differences between them?

▶▶

What set is this instrument in?

Percussion

A

?11 Look at these eight objects. Which one is not a musical instrument? Do you know what it is?

Ching

C Tock

D

Cr-r-r-r-r-r-r

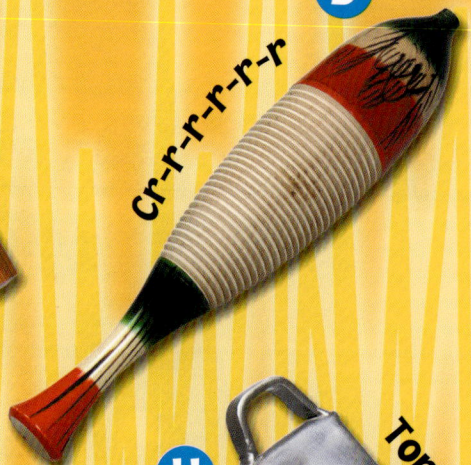

B Be-doyng

H Tonk

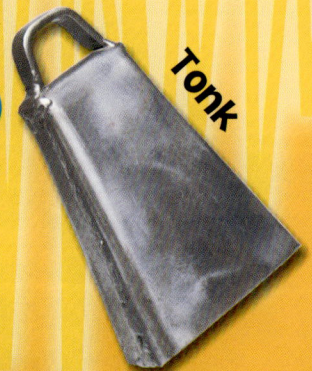

E

Tsh-sh-sh-sh-sh

F

Mmmmm

G Tcha-ka-taka-taka-tak

There are seven percussion instruments on page 10. Look at them and match them to the descriptions below.
Which one is which?

1 **Cow Bells**: deep bells, that could go round a cow's neck.

2 **Claves**: two bits of wood which you hit together to make a rhythm.

3 **Shakere**: a rattle covered with a net of beads.

4 **Rachet Rattle**: makes a rhythmic slapping sound as a piece of wood goes over a jagged wheel.

5 **Vibraslap**: makes a loud slap noise, followed by a **be-doyng!**

6 **Agogo Bells**: two bells click together as they are played by a stick

7 **Guiro**: makes a rhythmic, rasping sound when you rub a scraper along it.

▶▶

What kind of percussion instrument are these?

◀◀ Answer: They are bongo drums.

Drums

?13

This is a drum kit. How many drums are there? How many drums could the drummer play at once?

?14

This is an electronic drum machine. How is it different from the other drums?

drumsticks

timpani mallets

drum brushes

soft drum mallets

?15

Which of these sticks do you think would make the softest sound on a drum?

▶▶

What is this?

Wind

Brass

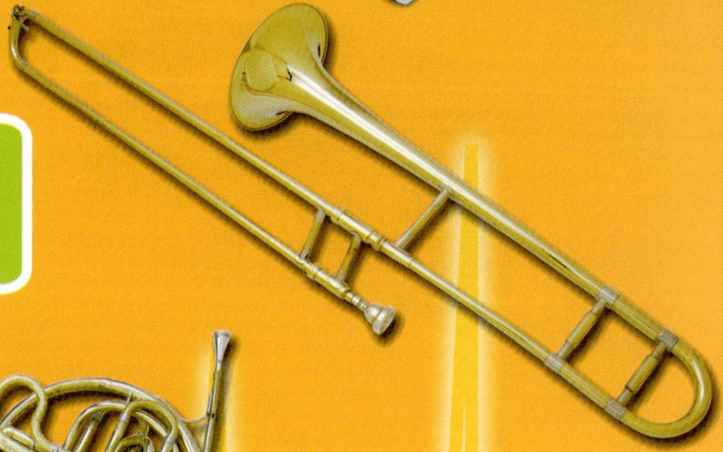

mouthpiece

keys

bell

?16

Look at these brass instruments. Which do you think this boy is playing?

14

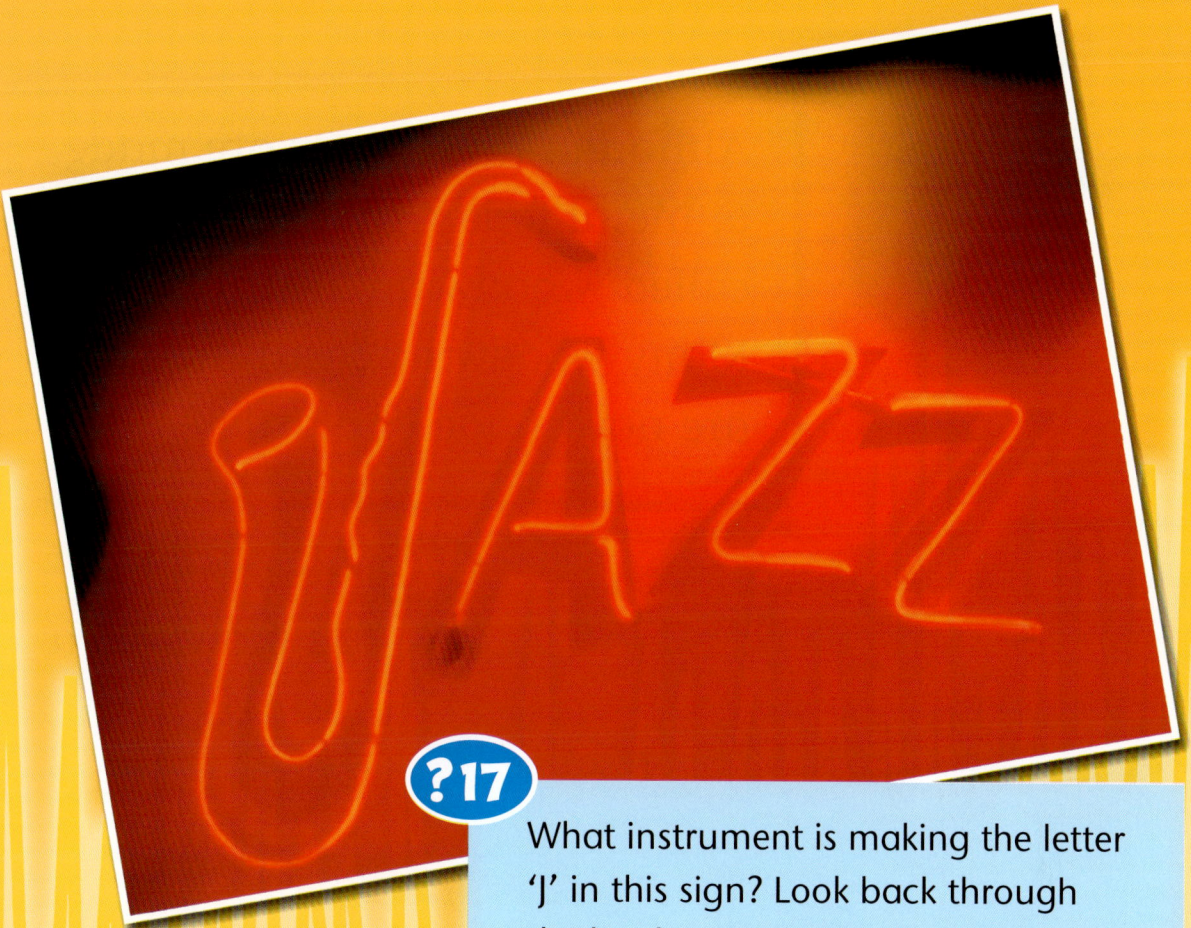

? 17

What instrument is making the letter 'J' in this sign? Look back through the book to compare the shape with all the instruments you've seen.

▶▶

One of these instruments is a flute and the other a saxophone. Which one is which?

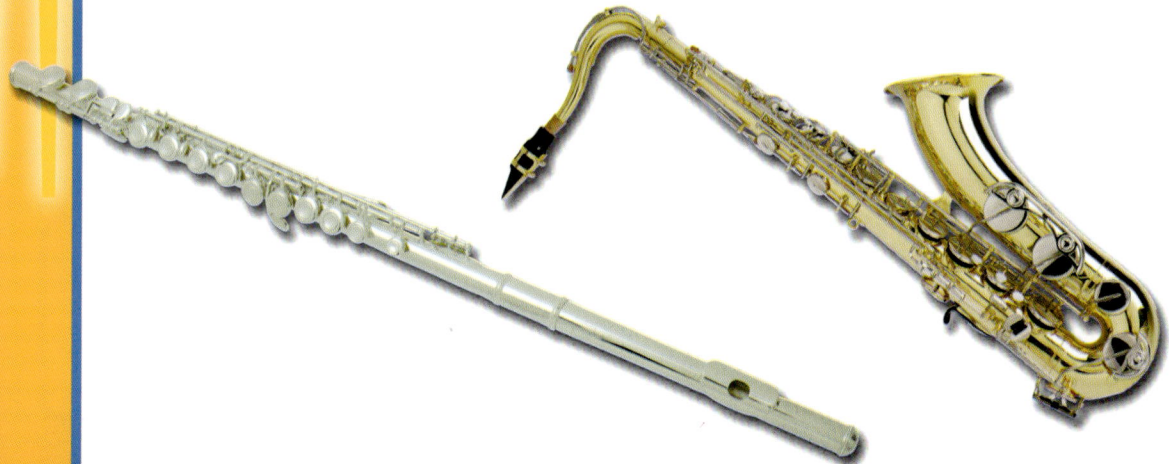

◀◀ Answer: The one on the left is the flute.

Wood

Although most flutes are made of metal today, they are still called 'woodwind' instruments. Many woodwind instruments are now made of plastic.

clarinet

flute

?18 You blow *into* a clarinet. How do you play a flute?

A

B

?19 Can you name these instruments? Have you played either of them?

bagpipe

horn

gourd flute

didgeridoo

?20 Can you guess which countries these wind instruments come from?

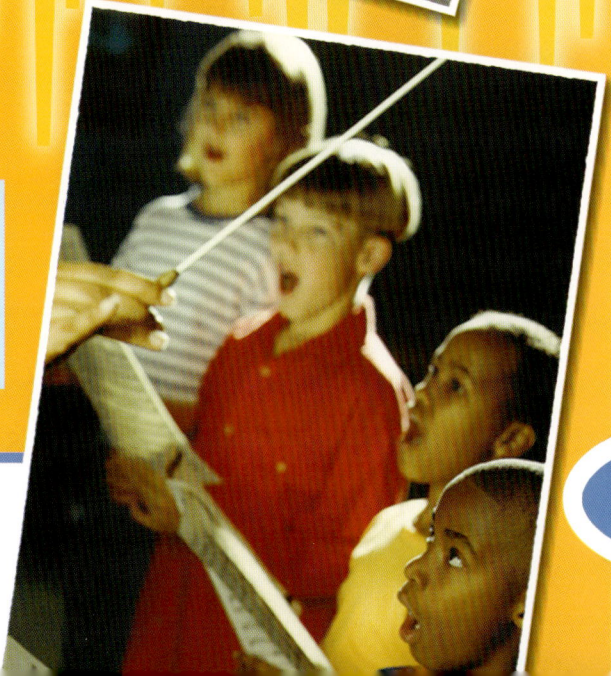

▶▶ What instrument do we always carry with us?

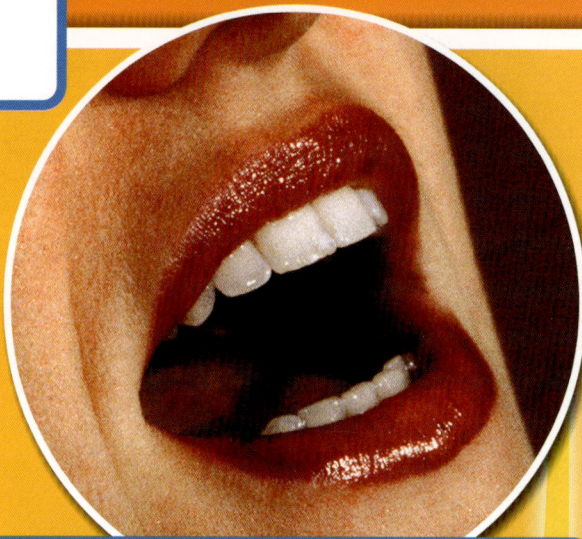

Voice

We can do lots of things with our voices.

We sing by passing air across our vocal cords, and the sound vibrates in our nose and mouth.

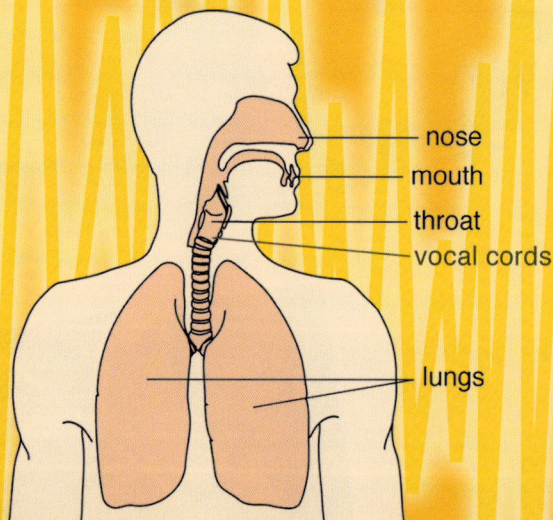

- nose
- mouth
- throat
- vocal cords
- lungs

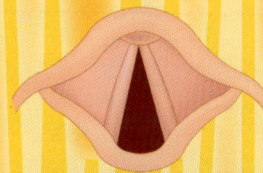

Loose cords

Tight cords

?21

Look at the diagrams of the vocal cords. Do you think the sound you make is higher or lower when the cords are loose?

?22

We can make our voices softer and louder too. Look at these soundwaves. Which shows a long, soft sound and which shows a quick, loud sound?

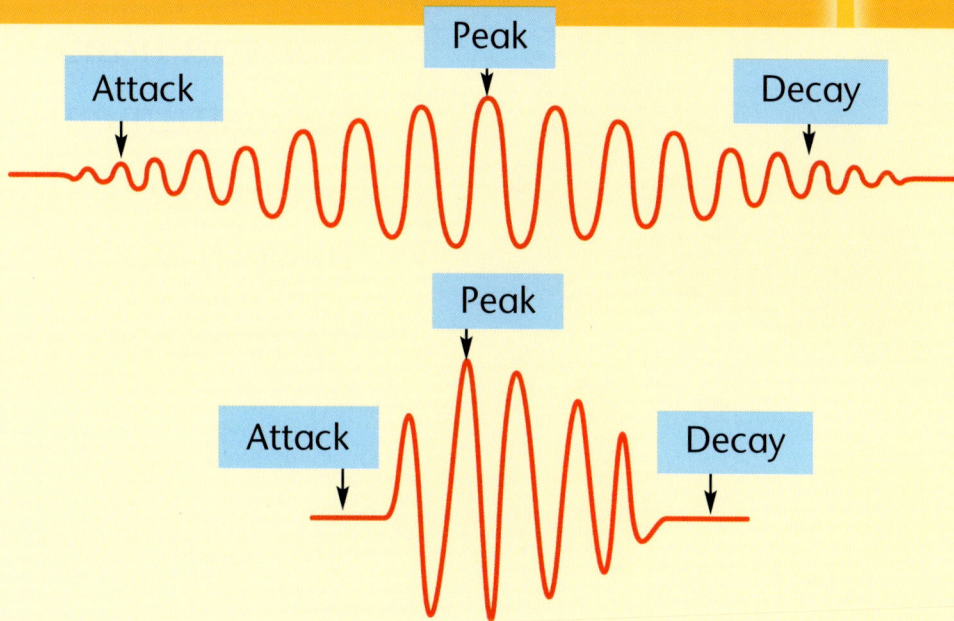

Peak

Attack

Decay

Peak

Attack

Decay

Can you sing or hum these two sounds? How do you know when to make your voice loud?

▶▶

What is the group name for a lot of people singing together?

19

◀◀ Answer: A Choir.

All Together Now!

?23

Can you name the instruments in this photo and put them in their sets?

?24

How many differents kinds of instruments can you see?

Music is often written for people to dance to.

Which concert would you rather be at?

▶▶

Which set would you put these spoons into?

Answers

Page 2 and 3

?1 The sound wave is from a snare drum.

Page 4 and 5

?2 The voice and some electronic instruments don't fit into these categories.

?3 The longest bar makes the lowest note. The shortest bar makes the highest note.

?4 The guitar is a string instrument. The Flutes are woodwind instruments. The tuba is a brass wind instrument

Page 6 and 7

?5 The sound gets lower

?6 The double bass makes the lowest sound and the violin makes the highest, because the strings are shorter and thinner.

?7 Bowing can make a longer sound than plucking.

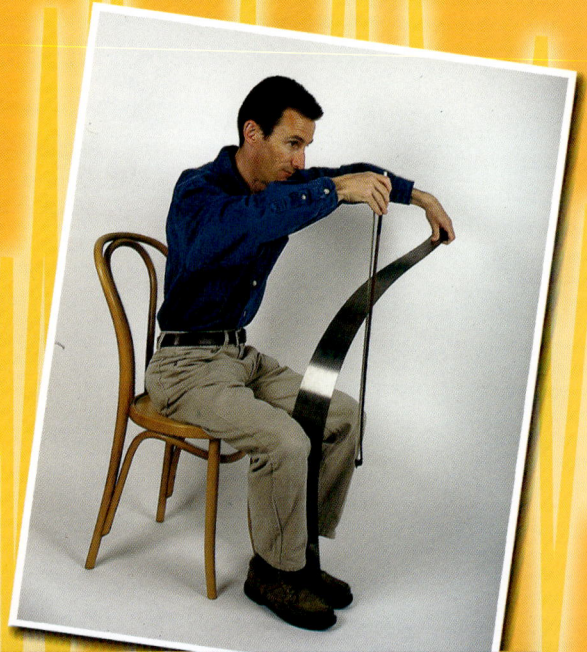

What instrument is this? It is being bowed, but it is not a string instrument.

Page 8 and 9

?8

Electric guitars numbers 2, 4 and 5

?9

The thick guitar is a folk guitar and the thin guitar is an electric one.

?10

The guitar on the right only has four strings. It is made for a left-handed player. The guitar on the left has six strings. It is for a right-handed player.

Page 10 and 11

?11

F, the tuning fork, is not an instrument. A tuning fork is used to help put a musical instrument in tune (at the correct musical pitch).

?12

A=6 (Agogo Bells),
B=5 (Vibraslap),
C=2 (Claves),
D=7 (Guiro),
E=3 (Shekere),
F=Tuning Fork,
G=4 (Ratchet rattle),
H=1 (Cow Bells)

Page 12 and 13

?13

There are 5 drums. The drummer can play 3 at one time. the big drum is played by a foot pedal.

?14

The electronic drum machine makes the noise electronically through speakers. It does not need a hollow space to make a noise.

?15

The brushes can make the quietest sound.

Page 14 and 15

?16

The boy is playing a trumpet.

?17

The J in the sign is a saxophone.

526877

Page 16 and 17

?18
You blow across the mouthpiece of a flute.

?19
B is a recorder. A is a kazoo.

?20
Bagpipe: Scotland, UK
Horn: Niger, Africa
Didgeridoo: Australia
Gourd Flute: India

Page 18 and 19

?21
Loose vocal cords make low notes.
Tight vocal cords make high notes.

?22
The first sound wave is a soft sound and the second is a loud sound

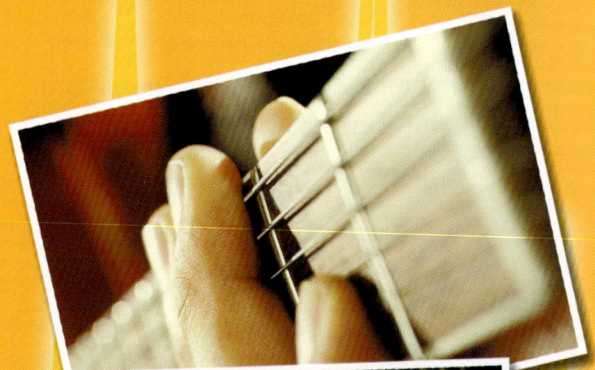

Page 20 and 21

?23
Flute (wind), violin (string-bowed) and triangle (percussion)

?24
French horns, tubas, trombones, trumpets.

Name the string instruments being played by these hands.